A Queen
Named King

Mary Virginia Fox

EAKIN PRESS ☆ Austin, Texas

STORIES FOR YOUNG AMERICANS

FIRST EDITION

Published in the United States of America
By Eakin Press, P.O. Box 23069, Austin, Texas 78735

ISBN 0-89015-562-3

Library of Congress Cataloging-in-Publication Data

Fox, Mary Virginia.
   A queen named king.

   Summary: A biography of Henrietta Chamberlain King, who helped build one of the world's largest cattle empires, the King Ranch in Texas.
      1. Chamberlain, Henrietta — Childhood and youth — Juvenile literature.
2. Ranchers — Texas — Biography — Juvenile literature. 3. King Ranch
(Tex.) — Juvenile literature. 4. Ranch life — Texas — Juvenile literature.
5. Texas — Biography — Juvenile literature.
   [1. Chamberlain, Henrietta. 2. Ranchers. 3. King Ranch (Tex.)]   I. Title.
F392.K47C423   1986   976.4 [B] [92]   86-16579
                  ISBN 0-89015-562-3

A Queen
Named King

Henrietta M. King

1

It was a strange way to meet a husband, their first words setting fire to an argument. Besides, Henrietta Chamberlain had not planned on getting married. She felt her life already had purpose. Most important, she prized her independence. But what happened that day in 1850 changed her whole life around.

Henrietta had stepped out on the deck of the *Whiteville* to catch a breath of fresher air. It was little better outside. The muddy, brown water of the Rio Grande added its own odor of rotting catfish that had been caught in the mud flats across from the dock.

She fanned herself with the apron she had tied around her cotton work skirt and checked the mooring line which held their floating home to shore. It was a strange home, but this was the only lodging the Reverend Chamberlain, Henrietta's father, had been able to find for his family. There were no houses to be rented in all of Brownsville, Texas.

Suddenly, a blast from the steam whistle of a river freighter tore through the air. This was followed by a torrent of words from the wheel house of the boat bearing down on them.

Although the exact words were never recorded, Henrietta remembered their meaning to be similar to, "For gawd's sake, who in the name of bejeesus has the green gall to tie that dang tub *Whiteville* in the way? Who?"

A man lounging on the dock looked up and grinned. He shouted a warning. "Don't know whether I'd talk that way hereabouts, Captain. The *Whiteville* is owned by a preacher now."

"A preacher? That's all I need, a sanctimonious reverend neighbor damning us all to perdition. Cast off that line and let loose that stinking rat trap."

Ordinarily, Henrietta would have primly and properly ignored the rough river captain, but she had just spent the last two hours on her knees scrubbing the deck and scuppers until they were spotless. Her anger matched his. She frowned at the sight of the shallow draft riverboat. The decks were loaded with a cargo of molasses barrels and a swarm of flies.

"And you, sir, are not a welcome visitor either. The *Whiteville* is a great sight, a very great sight, cleaner than," she squinted at the peeling letters on the side of the boat, "the *Colonel Cross*. And as for rats in the vicinity, I can guess where they are bred."

He was about to answer when she continued. "Your shameless, profane tongue is unfit for the ears of decent folks." She spun on her heels and ducked inside the fore cabin.

The riverboat captain was left speechless. His face turned an unaccustomed red. Meekly, he forced the engine against the suck and swirl of the mud-thick water and eased the vessel further on to another wharf.

Henrietta was seventeen but looked much older. She was slender, of medium height, but as one member of her family described her, she carried her head six feet above her shoulders. She wore her hair parted in the middle, pulled severely to a bun at the nape of her neck. Her huge brown eyes, which had been blazing at the captain's profanity, could glow with excitement or soften in tenderness.

Responsibility had been placed on her shoulders very early in life. Her own mother had died when Henrietta was three years old. Reverend Chamberlain had remarried, but no stepmother had quite been able to fill the role. Now three sons had been added to the family.

Henrietta idolized her father. Although a strict disciplinarian, he could do no wrong in her eyes. She wished at times she could be a man and step up to a pulpit, keeping a congregation spellbound as her father did.

Hiram Chamberlain was a man of education, unusual for a traveling minister who had never stayed in one place long enough to gather around him a permanent flock. He had graduated from Middlebury College and from Princeton Theological and Andover Theological Seminaries. He had a small inheritance that provided the family with modest means and adequate support to give Henrietta an education of sorts.

Education for women of the day was usually limited to the reading of sentimental poetry, an exposure to fine music, and perhaps an attempt at china painting. Henrietta was exposed to all these niceties when at fourteen she was sent away to the Female Institute in Holly Springs, Mississippi.

Henrietta recalled in later life that she felt something was missing. Her taste in reading material went far beyond poetry and the Bible. At times, her father would have been surprised to know how cosmopolitan her tastes had become. No, she did not share some of her schoolmates' forbidden romantic dime novels. She searched for heavier stuff: history, philosophy, world politics. Only a few volumes were available to her, and even then she had to search them out on the top shelves of the room that served as dining room and library.

She felt herself an outsider because her tastes were different. Every girl in school hoped soon to be married. What other future did they have? Henrietta wanted to be a teacher. At fourteen she was already teased as being a little old maid. It had nothing to do with her plainness. She was prettier than many beribboned and ruffled coquettes who might one day win that title against their wishes.

Henrietta was lonely and homesick at school. She wrote to her father asking to come home. His answering letter showed no sympathy. He urged her to rise above any unhappiness. "That will never do. It will injure your health and your mind . . . You were not made to be perfectly happy here. We must wait until we get to heaven for that."

For two years, Henrietta tried to follow her father's stern advice. It was a test of endurance. She returned home the summer of her sixteenth birthday to hear her father's news. They were moving to the "border," the southern tip of Texas. He was brimming with enthusiasm. He would carry the teachings of his faith to a new frontier.

Henrietta was caught up in the excitement. She might even be able to start a school for children of the new settlers who were coming to claim and settle the southern border of the thirty American states.

That's just what she did, but not without strong opposition. As soon as the Chamberlains were settled on their floating home, she went calling on the few families who were so adventurous or foolhardy, depending on whom you talked to, to think they could put down roots, rear children, and earn a living in such an uncivilized part of the country.

She enlisted a group of young people, both boys and girls, and set about organizing a broad curriculum she felt would be both practical and uplifting. Her idea to combine the sexes in the same classroom met strong disapproval.

Henrietta called on the parents, explaining her idea that young women, as well as young men, should receive the same fundamental education. Teaching boys and girls together gave both a more normal basis for discussion of ideals and goals in later life. Shocking, they said.

This was one of the few times Henrietta was forced to compromise. Rather than abandon her idea of a school altogether, she proposed to enroll young ladies only and give them the benefit of a liberal education — a better education than she had received in Holly Springs. She expected them to apply themselves diligently five and a half days a week.

It had been on a Saturday afternoon that she had had her words with the captain. Having become used to some of the tough characters on the Mexican-American frontier, her anger had subsided, and she had put the captain out of her mind.

5

3

It was the captain who remembered the encounter much more vividly. He was a bit ashamed that he had blown his steam valve shouting at her. It had been a rough six-day trip from Boca del Rio on the Gulf upriver to Camargo with wooding stops along the way, and four days back down the current to Brownsville. The heat had been stifling. That's what had set off his temper, he told himself. He even considered apologizing to the young lady sometime.

The crew unloading his boat that afternoon hid a grin or two and voiced the sentiment that no one else on the river could have taken over Captain King's docking space without a brawling, skull-splitting battle. Not only that, since docking, the captain had been uncommonly quiet, giving few orders and retiring to his cabin.

That was one of the reasons his friend and partner, Mifflin Kenedy, had searched him out.

"I expected you yesterday, Richard. Run into some kind of trouble?"

When the captain answered, the quiet of the after-

6

noon quickly wore off. "You're right, there's something wrong, and it starts with this dang clinker that's too light for the outside sea run and too heavy for the bed of dew I've been navigating."

"And just what would you have me do about it?"

"Order up two new boats, one a big stout side-wheeler built to stand ocean water and carry payloads from the Gulf upriver as far as possible. A decent terminal should be built at White Ranch to handle transfer of cargo to a lightweight, flat-bottom mud skimmer. Give her some kicking boilers, and I'll bet you a year's wages that we'll knock out all competition afloat."

"That'll take cash, Richard."

"Credit, Mifflin. This river has nothing but rotten tugs that will crack on the first blow in from the Gulf, which reminds me," he assumed a casual tone, "what do you know about the new preacher over there on the *Whiteville*?"

"Seems to be a sober and godly man," Kenedy answered. "He plans to establish the first Protestant church on the border."

"Which I expect brings approval from a Quaker like you."

Kenedy nodded.

"About his family, have you met them?"

"Yes, a splendid wife."

"And children?"

Kenedy smiled to himself. It was obvious about whom the questions were directed, but he delighted in seeing his friend squirm. "Three sons, one an infant."

"No daughters?"

"Oh yes, I'd forgotten. Miss Henrietta Marie Morse Chamberlain, age seventeen, I believe."

It was the first time he had ever seen Richard King at a loss for words. Finally, after a long hesitation, the gruff captain asked, "Would you find a time to introduce me, Mifflin?"

Kenedy smiled. "Why of course, Richard, that is, if you will accompany me to a prayer meeting and church social aboard the *Whiteville* next Wednesday evening."

"We'll see," was all that King would promise. He would be as out of place as a rattler in a fish net, but he was determined to meet the girl with spirit.

4

In spite of extreme nervous discomfort, he and Mifflin attended the Wednesday prayer meeting. Henrietta recognized him immediately. He was a big man with square shoulders, a square jaw, and square powerful hands. His handshake numbed her fingers. There was no mention of their original encounter. This was the time for an apology, but the words stuck in his throat.

He fidgeted through the sermon, but when the break came to mingle with the congregation, he shed all his shyness and engaged Miss Henrietta in conversation for the rest of the evening.

She asked him how long he had been a riverboat pilot, and from there on the captain was on familiar ground, the story of his life, which he promptly unfolded chapter by chapter.

He had been born of Irish immigrant parents in the city of New York. At nine he had been apprenticed to a jeweler. He had hated the trade, and at eleven had escaped as a stowaway aboard the ship *Desdemona* bound through the straits, up the coast of Florida to sunny Mobile Bay. The ship's captain had befriended him and, before leaving port, had arranged for King to be hired as a steamship "cub" on the Alabama River. He had stayed on to earn his own pilot's license.

"And how did you happen to reach this seemingly out of the way port?" Henrietta asked.

"The war, Ma'am, the war. Captain Kenedy, who accompanied me this evening" — hadn't it been the other way around? — "was pressed into service to provide transport for our troops fighting in Mexico. He was in need of an experienced riverman. Naturally, he called upon me."

Henrietta listened attentively. She had to admit she was impressed, not only by his rather handsome face and bearing, but by his enthusiasm for life. Modesty was surely not one of his faults. He owned his own boat, well half a share of it, and had plans for future expansion. She liked hearing his ideas. It was so much more interesting than the chatter she was used to.

King and Kenedy were the last ones to leave. Henrietta invited them to attend services in the near future. King vowed that he would try.

Business on the river kept him away from Brownsville for long periods of time, but he did attend several church meetings. The Reverend Chamberlain was not at all impressed with the burly young riverman — captain or not — seeking the refined company of his daughter who had dedicated her life, he thought, to the furthering of Christian teaching.

However, there was very little he could do to keep them apart when the young man chose to attend services. Besides, Henrietta had a mind of her own. Hadn't her father taught her that a girl did not have to be a "clinging vine?" She could "master her own destiny," he had written in one of his letters. She found Captain King's visits an exciting diversion in a life that had already found a rut of monotony.

Richard King's life was far from that. Profits were

10

mounting. More people were pouring into the southern tip of Texas along the Rio Grande. More people meant more commerce. Two new boats, the *Grampus* and *Comanche* had been added to the line. They had been built in Pittsburg to the captain's exact specifications.

Young King had his eyes on the future, yet his knowledge of the land around him was only what he had been able to see from the wheel house of a riverboat. When he heard that the settlement of Corpus Christi was planning an extravaganza, calling it the "Lone Star Fair," he decided to attend. Advance publicity promised "circus and theatrical performances, contests in riding and tailing wild bulls, fireworks, cock fights, and lectures on philosophy and literature."

King chose to make the trip by land. It would give him a chance to see what the country was really like. The map told him it was a journey of some 170 miles, but nothing could have prepared him for the wildness of the scenery, as well as its beauty.

He was lucky to have joined two other travelers who knew the way well. Otherwise, he might have been lost within an hour after leaving the Rio Grande. Winding through palmetto thickets, the road soon led over lowlands of dry grass and snaggy chaparral to the sandbanks of the Arroyo Colorado. Twelve miles beyond, they came to a camping place at the crumbled huts of a deserted ranch.

There was a brooding loneliness to the sweep of prairie. The flat sky was broken only occasionally by a gray line of live oak, but the prairie was not deserted. There were herds of wild horses, antelope, and deer. Turkey flocks whirred into the air as they passed.

After 124 miles of hard riding, the road led through stirrup-high grass nourished by the fresh water of the Santa Gertrudis stream. Forty-five miles farther on across a black loam flatland lay Corpus Christi, a frontier town of fewer than 500 inhabitants — when not multiplied by the transients who had come to the fair.

11

It is certain the Reverend Chamberlain and Henrietta would have disapproved of the rowdy carnival atmosphere. Whiskey was cheaper than barreled drinking water, and many felt the need for economy. But before leaving the fair, Captain King set in motion a legal transaction to own some of the property he had just seen. He was given advice both for and against the action.

Jeth Johnson, a lawyer he consulted, assured him, "Yes, I can promise you a legal purchase of land. Now that the U.S. border has been shoved south, most of the Mexican families hereabouts have abandoned their holdings. But the Texas legislature has agreed to guarantee title of the original Spanish land grants. What are you looking for?"

"I saw some mighty fine grassland for cattle," King answered.

An interested bystander interrupted. "Listen, Captain, land and livestock ain't no good unless you got an army to protect them from Indians and hide peelers and horse thieves."

"Well, I might just enlist my own cavalry," was King's answer. And he set about doing just that.

He had met a young man his age who was anxious to invest in the future. His name was Gideon Lewis, but most people called him Legs Lewis. He had recently been appointed captain of the company of Texas Mounted Volunteers that patrolled and protected the area around Corpus Christi.

King approached Lewis with the idea of going into partnership. Lewis agreed, expecting the river captain would be a silent partner. He couldn't have been more wrong. What King owned, he planned to manage.

The captain's first parcel of land at the fork formed by the Santa Gertrudis and the San Fernando creeks was purchased for the sum of $300. This included 15,500 acres of grazing land, averaging a little less than two cents an acre. The date was July 25, 1853.

When word spread that some crazy riverman was

paying cash for tracts in the Wild Horse Desert, sometimes known as the Desert of the Dead, all sorts of offers of land came his way. Within a year, Lewis and King had added 53,000 acres of grass for the total consideration of $1,800.

Now came the business of developing these assets. There were no examples to follow. The *gringos* from the north came as farmers, but this land was too dry for crops. The Mexicans from the south had been rounding up wild herds of cattle from the range for the past 150 years. But the only cattle known to survive in the harsh environment were Texas Longhorns. These animals were lanky as deer, with snaky horns extending sometimes eight or nine feet from tip to tip. Only hides and tallow were valuable. The meat was useless because without refrigeration there was no way to get it from remote range lands to city centers. Besides, the stringy beef was so tough, no matter how butchered or cooked, few thought it would ever sell well.

King had other ideas. He confided in Henrietta on one of his stops in Brownsville. "If we can improve herds, I'll find a way to get them to market."

"Can't they be sent by ship?" Henrietta suggested.

"You couldn't transport that many live animals, and butchered meat would spoil. What I propose is to drive them all the way to Kansas City and sell them on the hoof. You can't sell fresher meat than that."

"Does that mean you're giving up the steamship line?" she asked with interest. If he abandoned his life on the river she might see him in Brownsville more often. She had to admit that during the past months (which had added up to years, four in all, since the Chamberlains had moved to the border) she looked forward to seeing him. She grew impatient when his business kept him away for weeks at a time.

No romantic ties had developed, but a strong friendship was there. He was such a vital person, on the run to step into the future. It was impossible for him to carry on a dull conversation. He shared his dreams with her, and she shared his enthusiasm.

When he did answer her question, it was with a swing in both directions. "No, I won't be giving up the river, not entirely, but I've been noticing that land and livestock have been increasing in value. Buy boats and they have a way of wrecking, decaying, and falling apart. Land is where the future lies."

Following his own advice, he spent most of his time at the ranch, rather than in the offices of the shipping line. Henrietta saw less of him than ever. Now that King owned land, he set about improving his stock as best he knew how. First, he had to find trained cattle handlers. Mexican *vaqueros* were the answer, men more at home on horse than on foot. They rode strong-legged, tender-mouthed horses that seemed to know without prodding just what their riders wanted.

Men had to be housed when they weren't on the range. King hired Francisco Alvarado from a neighboring ranch to be in charge of all building. *Jacales,* houses of wood and dirt with roofs of thatch, were quickly erected. Workers fenced in corrals with thorny mesquite, the only cheap lumber around. They dug water tanks and lined them with layers of a wiry evergreen grass that grew in the area to keep the water from seeping away in the sandy soil.

A rough stockade and blockhouse were built. A war surplus cannon was freighted in and mounted in the compound, more to frighten off enemies than to be used in actual warfare.

Captains James Richardson and William Gregory, both veterans of the Mexican War, were put in charge of defenses. Two of Captain King's river crew, Vincent Patino and Faustino Villa, made up the rest of the standing army to supplement the help King expected from Legs Lewis's regular troops.

Now it was time to stock the ranch. From Mexico King bought his first cows and a cinnamon-colored bull.

14

He also sought out the best bloodlines available to up-
breed his stock. The same year he spent $300 for the
whole of the Santa Gertrudis tract, he paid $600 for one
sorrel stud named Whirlpool.

He did not sell any of his stock at first. He was busy
building up his herd. The news spread fast, which
brought a welcome cattle boom to the cow towns of Camargo and Mier. Ranchers on the border drove herds in
from thirsty ranges. King bought the stock and sent
them to pastures farther north of the Rio Grande.

Henrietta heard news of his dealings from those who
passed through Brownsville, but it was months before
she heard the details from Richard himself. When he did
come to town, he first asked to see Reverend Chamberlain. He had decided it was time to settle down and raise
a family. He had long ago chosen Henrietta as his in-
tended, although he had failed to mention it to her,
thinking she knew all along how much he needed her.
She was a strong woman, a compassionate one. He knew
by the way she helped the families of her students when
they were in need. And he could talk with her as an
equal. No woman he had known before had so many fine
qualities.

King outlined his plans first to Hiram Chamberlain.
He was never one to suffer from false modesty, so that
when he spoke of his present holdings, he incorporated
some of his future plans. The cow camp was made to
sound like an established town outshining the growing
center of Brownsville.

Reverend Chamberlain had little doubt that King
would be able to support his daughter in style, but would
it be in Christian style? He was glad to hear that King
planned to turn over most of the riverboat business to
Kenedy. The roustabouts and crew men were a rough lot.
He hadn't noticed that the cowmen of the day were earn-
ing a worse reputation. The preacher hesitated in giving
his answer, but when Henrietta heard of the proposal, it
was she who made the decision. She accepted.

15

On December 9, 1854, the county clerk of Cameron County issued a license to join Miss Henrietta Maria Morse Chamberlain and Captain Richard King in the bond of matrimony.

At the evening service in the recently erected Presbyterian church, Henrietta sat in her accustomed place in the choir; Captain King was in the front pew before her. The service seemed endless to both of them. More than once, Henrietta glanced up from her hymnal to survey with approval the chin whiskers the captain had recently grown. He, in turn, stared in awe at the fashionable young woman who by far outshown others in the congregation. The dress she wore was of peach-colored ruffled silk, with a front of white silk mull "shirred and trimmed with beading and white baby ribbons under sleeves of white lace."

Henrietta would surely bring distinction to the kingdom the captain was establishing between the Nueces River and the Rio Grande.

5

Few brides ever had such royal treatment on their honeymoon. Captain King had purchased a private stagecoach at a price of $400 for their four-day trip to the Santa Gertrudis ranch. Armed outriders kept pace with the coach during the day and stood guard over the camp at night.

The cook had his pack horse loaded with provisions and utensils. The bride's trousseau, which included not only her clothing but linens, a few pieces of family silver, and a box of books, was packed in a buckboard guarded by two men with shotguns.

No luxury was spared that could be provided, but it must have been a strange wedding night for Henrietta bedded down beside the coals of a campfire, hearing the howls of coyotes on the prairie and the snorting of horses tethered tightly in a circle (lest Indians or rustlers break them loose to strand the wedding party in the middle of the Desert of the Dead).

But Henrietta had no misgivings. She was in love.

She was happy. She was excited. She had surely moved out of her rut, and the future could only hold promise.

Still, she was surprised at what she saw. The land through which they were traveling was so different from the picture Richard King had given her. A drought had plagued the entire West that year. The lush grass of the range had shriveled and died. The mud from the few watering sinks had turned to white dust that was churned by the riders into choking clouds.

"It's worse than I thought," King admitted, "but don't worry, Etta, the rains will come and overnight this will be transformed into an Eden."

Henrietta smiled. "It's good, Captain, to hear you are familiar with the Bible."

He grinned. "Dear Etta, don't expect complete conversion, but I am trying."

She liked the nickname he had chosen for her, but Captain was what she called her Richard all of his life.

Tomorrow they would be at the ranch. Tomorrow they would close their door and the world outside would wait for them. That was as she dreamed it. It was not to be so.

Captains Lewis, Richardson, and Gregory were waiting for them when they drove up. A dozen brown-faced *vaqueros* lined in military precision were at the door of the little ranch house that was to be their home. Greetings were exchanged, and the couple entered the house hand in hand. Richard King stood nervously watching his bride survey the three rooms furnished with rough, hand-hewn furniture. What had seemed adequate before now looked crude and ugly to him.

"This is just the beginning, Etta. I will build you a mansion."

"I don't need a mansion, Captain," she laughed, "just a larger pantry."

"Alvarado will help you. Plan what you want. The space under this roof is cramped, but when you've rested I want to show you what else you own."

"Let's go look." Eagerly she went outside again.

Two horses were saddled and waiting for them. It was Henrietta's turn to be nervous.

"You do ride, don't you?" King asked.

Henrietta nodded. "Yes, but always sidesaddle." She took a deep breath. "Don't worry, I'll manage."

She was dressed in a full calico skirt, muslin petticoat, and enough ruffles on her knee-length pantaloons to conceal all but an ankle. As she mounted her horse, she vowed that she would remodel a dress into a more convenient riding outfit.

"We'll only be able to circle the nearest fence line. You won't have much chance to judge the land today, but you'll come to recognize the sections. We have sparse sand range, but here at the Santa Gertrudis the sod is thick and we can have a season or more of drought that won't kill roots. We're going to be damming up more reservoirs as we increase the herds."

Henrietta was proud he was sharing his ideas with her. At first he kept his horse reined in to stay abreast her mount, but as he tested her ability in the saddle, he led the way at a loping gallop. Henrietta hugged her knees against the horse's sides and took the jolts as best she could by tensing against the stirrups. She would learn to ride well, but today she was glad to see them head back to the corral after only a short survey.

Henrietta found that if she were to be with her husband when he was here on the ranch she would have to spend time in the saddle. She made herself a divided corduroy skirt. King immediately ordered boots in her size. She objected at first, saying she felt more ladylike in her buttoned shoes, but she soon learned that the shape of a western boot was made to slide easily into a stirrup, and the tough leather was good protection whenever they rode into the brush.

Every day, the captain made inspection rounds. Whenever he was only a day's ride from the house, she went along. It took more than a month to cover all the

19

range they owned. Property lines on the far sections were defined only by a few stakes. Cattle roamed at will. That was why during the heaviest calving time it was important to brand the animals.

Richard King, though rough and tough with others, was tender and caring with Henrietta. When the weather was oven-hot and he thought she was tiring on their rides across the prairie, he would spread a Mexican blanket under the shade of a mesquite tree so that she could rest. It was then he would talk of his plans, of the stock he had bought, of his dream to deliver live beef all the way to Kansas City. He talked to her as a business partner. When he was away from the ranch, he let it be known that she was to be consulted on all matters.

She was always busy, and yet she was a woman alone surrounded by people. She proved to be a remarkably self-sufficient frontier wife, perhaps because she had never before settled long enough in one place to depend on friends for entertainment or confidences.

There were none like her on the frontier. She was a woman of considerable education, a taste for at least some of the arts, music and books, and a church background that had little in common with the fiesta mood of Mexican Catholicism. The ranch workers, called *Kiñenos* or King's people, were devoted to their church and their priest, but it was the pomp and pageantry that drew many of them to God. Henrietta's principles were more Puritan: no levity, no drinking, Sundays spent in pious reading of the Lord's word. Her husband respected her way of life, but did not join her. Religion caught up with him only when they were in Brownsville, when he attended the services conducted by his father-in-law.

Although she called on all the families living on the ranch, her station in life set her apart. The *Kiñenos* called her "La Madama" or "La Patrona" with a respectful bow. She learned their language and came to them with medicine when they were ill, but who could she read poetry with?

Her reputation as a healer came quite by accident. She had dropped by the one-room adobe house of Anselmo Flores. His wife had recently given birth to their first child. The young mother was alone and frantic with worry. The baby was having trouble breathing. It would take days before a doctor could be summoned from town.

Henrietta remembered her stepmother ministering to one of the boys who had a bad case of croup. A steam kettle with a drop of turpentine had helped. Now it was worth a try.

She set the kettle to boiling and held the infant in her arms until normal breathing returned. Henrietta never knew whether her primitive treatment had helped, but Maria Flores regarded her as a saint.

From that time on, Henrietta was summoned for all emergencies. Little by little, she learned to cope with a variety of ailments. She had to. It was not until much later in the history of the King ranch that professional medical care was available.

Their house was extremely modest by any standards, but the King reputation as generous hosts was legend. Anyone passing through, whether a cowhand or a famous guest, was treated to the best food and lodging the frontier could offer. Richard King's closest friend, Legs Lewis, the one who shared his partnership in the ranch, made frequent stops.

It was a deep shock to them when they heard of his death. Lewis was shot in Corpus Christi by a jealous husband. No doubt Henrietta was upset by the scandal, but she had come to look forward to his visits. He provided the humorous tidbits of news which were a longtime making their way out to the ranch.

This not only left King without a friend and adviser, it left him without a clear title to the ranch. Lewis had left no will, and King had no money to purchase his share. Profits from the steamship line had long ago been used to stock the ranch. His credit was already strained, yet he had no intention of allowing the Lewis holdings to pass into strange hands.

His greatest assets were his friends. King made arrangements with a close associate, Major William Chapman, to present a bid on the property at the court-ordered public sale. The top bid was $1,575. Arrangements were made by King's lawyer that payment would be delayed one year from the date of purchase. Cash was always scarce on the frontier.

King depended heavily on the skill of lawyer Stephen Powers of Brownsville. King had learned that a good lawyer was a necessity. Early land grants frequently left a tangle of titles, but none of King's cattle-buying contracts or property titles were ever questioned in court. He made sure of that.

6

More and more of the captain's time was spent in town handling business transactions. He hated to leave Henrietta alone, although there is no record, even in her letters, that she ever voiced a complaint. But she was pleased when he came up with a suggestion.

"I think we need two houses, Etta. I was talking to Mifflin Kenedy the other day. It's been two years since he and his bride settled on Elizabeth Street in Brownsville. They've asked us to drop by and see them. If you like the idea, I'll make inquiries and see if we can't find ourselves a building lot."

Immediately, property was purchased next door to the Kenedys, and a builder was engaged. The planning was left to Henrietta.

Their Elizabeth Street neighbors, dubbed the Brick House Crowd, were all affluent citizens who owned businesses and property holdings in the area. Brownsville had flourished and grown since the days Henrietta had spent aboard the *Whiteville*.

The Chamberlains had settled into a home of their

own, and Henrietta enjoyed spending time with her father and her stepfamily. Even the captain was welcome and now much admired by his in-laws. King was careful to smooth over the roughest of his speech, and orange juice took the place of his preferred Red Eye whiskey.

Although the Kings had many pleasant times with their friends in town, they rarely were seen at the Brownsville opera or social functions of the army set. Neither the captain nor Henrietta cared to hobnob with the Brownsville society for the sake of gaining favors. It was Brownsville society who knocked on their doors in vain.

One of their frequent guests was Col. Robert E. Lee. Lee and King had met on one of the river steamers. Lee was impressed and interested in the captain's accounts of ranching activities. Being a farmer himself, he asked permission to visit the Santa Gertrudis ranch.

"First you must come stay with us in town. Then I'll ride out to the ranch with you," King suggested.

Lee later wrote to his wife, "The King home was removed from the street by well-kept trees and shrubbery in the yard, among which were several orange trees filled with ripening fruit. Mrs. King's table was loaded with sweet oranges and many other things tempting to the eye."

The next day the two men started out on horseback to make a tour of the ranch. Lee was amazed at the limitless expanse of the grasslands.

"You could feed the world from here, Captain. My advice is, buy land and never sell," said Lee.

"This is only the beginning," King assured him. "The main house will be built soon."

"That would make a fine site," said Lee, pointing to the slight rise of land at the fork of the two streams.

That was exactly where the ranch house was built.

A month later, Lee returned and asked again to see the ranch. He was considering a similar investment himself. King made arrangements for someone else to accompany him. He didn't want to leave Henrietta this time. She was expecting a baby.

She was in perfect health and close to fine medical help, but the captain cancelled all out-of-town business and spent the better part of each day, so it seemed to Henrietta, inquiring, "How are you feeling, Etta? Any sign yet?"

The nursery was furnished with cradle and hand-woven coverlet. There was no more anxious or proud father-to-be than Richard King. His friend and neighbor Mifflin Kenedy joshed him.

"You'd best spend more time at the steamship office, Richard, or you'll wear out the carpet as well as Henrietta's nerves."

Finally, on April 17, 1856, their daughter was born. She was promptly baptized by her grandfather and christened Henrietta Maria King, nicknamed Nettie.

King had been all too inactive these past few weeks. Now he threw himself into both projects, ranching and river freighting. Contracts had been signed with the quartermaster of the army, General Jesup, to supply mules, horses, feed, and commissary supplies. Both interests profited.

Soon the captain was shuttling back and forth between the ranch and Brownsville. He tried to discourage Henrietta from making the trip with the baby, but she missed the ranch and wanted to be with him.

When little Nettie was about six months old, they left Brownsville on the familiar 124-mile trip. They went by carriage, traveling light without the security guard that would have been provided if they were transporting any of their belongings.

In the evening, when they were camping by the side of the road, a lone Mexican rider approached them and asked permission to join them for the night. King agreed reluctantly. The stranger thanked them and unsaddled his horse. King was busy starting a fire. Henrietta had spread a blanket on the ground and was tending to Nettie. She looked up to say something to her husband and gasped. The man was creeping toward King with knife in hand.

"Captain, behind you!" she shouted.

In one sweeping motion, King spun and caught the man's arm. He jerked the man up and over, slamming him to the ground on his back. King reached for his gun, a shotgun loaded with buckshot.

"Now bygawd, get your ass out of here."

The man ran. King turned back to the fire as if nothing very unusual had happened. "Excuse me, Etta. I lost my temper. Now we can set about cooking our supper."

It was some time before Henrietta regained her breath.

Roving bandits were not the only danger a frontier wife and mother had to fear. One day, Henrietta was setting out bread in the kitchen while little Nettie slept in her cradle.

"I had a strange feeling somebody was standing behind me," Henrietta said later. She was right. When she turned, there by the cradle was an Indian with a club in his hand. As casually as she could manage, she picked up a loaf of freshly baked bread and handed it to him. He hesitated, then pointed to the other loaves. Henrietta rushed to load his arms with all he could carry. The war club was put back in his belt and he left as silently as he had come.

When King heard what had happened, he issued orders to have a guard at the house at all times. For a while it was a comfort, but later a nuisance. "I'm sure I can take care of any emergency, Captain. I know you are never far away," Henrietta insisted.

But he was. King was frequently away from the ranch on business. He urged her to return to their Brownsville home. She declined.

"In town I just fritter my time away."

He smiled. "Dear Etta, what you call idleness is full-scale work for most women."

26

Only during pregnancy did Henrietta give up her rigorous schedule of watching over ranch activities as well as household tasks. On April 13, 1858, a second daughter was born, named Ella Morse King. The captain may have been disappointed he still had no son, but no one would have known. Little Ella was shown off with the same pride as her older sister. In fact, Henrietta's only worry was that he would surely spoil the children.

Almost immediately, she returned to the ranch. "I can keep an eye on things when you are gone."

She did. Even when King was not around to go with her, Henrietta often rode out on the range to inspect the herds. When she was gone, the children were taken care of by Maria Flores.

Henrietta took special pride in the fact that the captain had registered a special brand in her name. The HK was listed as belonging to Mistress Henrietta M. King. It was some time later that the famous running W [   ] brand came into being.

The first livestock to be sold from the ranch were horses and mules. At a time when livestock had to be driven, not shipped, to market, it was easier to make delivery of animals that could be ridden. When some of the ranch's cattle were put up for sale, only selected breeding stock was disposed of to other ranchers. A few animals eliminated from the herds to improve the breed were slaughtered for their hides and tallow, but the problem of how to ship meat to distant markets still had not been solved.

King tried preserving carcasses, not merely by salting down chunks of beef but by injecting brine solution into the veins of whole sides of slaughtered beef. This definitely did not enhance the taste of the product, so King abandoned the idea. He still envisioned the possibility of herding cattle to markets more than a thousand miles away. He tried to interest other ranchers in the possibility of buying a corridor of land through the whole state of

Texas. It would have been extremely expensive, and no one quite believed that cattle could be herded that far.

To escape the heat of the summer of 1859, King decided to take his family north on a combination vacation and business trip. Henrietta's half brother, Hiram Chamberlain, Jr., accompanied them. He had plans to attend college in Danville, Kentucky, and the captain was in the market for good thoroughbred horses. They could not have picked a better time to be away from Texas. Trouble was brewing.

7

For many years, and with good reason, feelings between Mexicans and Americans on the border had been far from friendly. Many Mexicans felt their land had been stolen by the United States. It didn't take much prodding for feelings to explode into violence.

A leader, Juan Cortina, appeared who stirred up this race hatred. Gathering a force of some 500 to 700 renegades, he swept across the land bordering the Rio Grande, plundering and murdering whoever blocked their way. In late September of 1859, they captured the city of Brownsville and set fire to many of the buildings. It was not until the new commander of the Eighth Military Department, Col. Robert E. Lee, led an attacking force that U.S. troops brought order to the banks of the Rio Grande.

The King ranch had not been touched, but many head of cattle had been driven across the border. What worried King even more was the constant rumor that a civil war to the north was brewing. The state of Texas was losing no time organizing for war, so were the partners of King and Kenedy. They set about consolidating their ranching and freighting business. Kenedy now owned large tracts of range land that bordered the Santa Gertrudis spread. If war came, the army would need their services both for supplies and transport. They ordered new boats for the increased river traffic they expected. Shipyards were in the north. They had to buy those boats before traffic was completely cut off.

King spent more time in Brownsville now, and Henrietta went with him. She was expecting their third child. On December 15, 1860, Richard King, Jr., was born. King's enthusiasm was boundless. He loved his daughters, but he needed a son to take over the management of the ranch some day.

It was at this time Henrietta decided they should part with their home on Elizabeth Street. "Our home is at the ranch. Now I feel torn between two lives, but our children must grow up to love the land, to know it as we do."

King gladly agreed. Only Henrietta's father was disappointed to see them go. He wrote, "I am truly sorry to part with them. But I suppose it is all for the best. This is a world of changes."

There were changes of all kinds. Suddenly, the mouth of the Rio Grande became the Confederacy's back door. The South needed cash to supply the army. Currency came in the shape of 500-pound bales of cotton that had to be delivered across the border. The Union had successfully blockaded Southern ports, but there was nothing they could do to intercept foreign ships in Mexican waters.

Six thousand or more pounds of cotton were piled on each rocking, dust-covered wagon that moved across the King ranch. Every day the stream grew longer. Here the teamsters and brokers' agents stopped to buy camp supplies, horses, mules, and beef, for the last leg of the journey to the border.

King became a speculative cotton buyer himself. The ranch headquarters of the Santa Gertrudis was an official receiving, storage, and shipping point. Although there is no doubt King made a personal profit on most transactions, he earned the prize. He kept the cotton trains rolling past the Yankee patrols and border thieves, and he delivered many supplies to the Confederate army on credit, paying for them with his own funds.

Some supplies were still loaded onto King and Kenedy river steamers, but to keep these boats out of the hands of the Yankees, the ships' registry was changed to the country of Mexico. Northern generals realized that something had to be done to pinch off the last line of commerce in the South.

More and more raiding parties were sent into southern Texas. Henrietta tried to keep life on the ranch as normal as possible for her family. Livestock had to be cared for, as well as the growing number of people who made the trail south into a highway. Yes, she had help, but without efficient organization there would have been chaos.

The captain was with her some of the time, but he was in the saddle more than at home. No place, not even the Santa Gertrudis ranch, remained safe.

On April 29, 1862, in the midst of the danger, a little girl was born at the ranch house built on the rise above the creek, the site Robert E. Lee had suggested. She was christened Alice Gertrudis King.

She was a solemn little bundle. Her eyes soon turned the deep brown of Henrietta's. From the beginning, people noted the resemblance. As always, King showed immense pride in his growing family, bragging to anyone who would listen of each one's accomplishments. But he had little time to bounce them on his knee or take them riding on the range that could any day turn into a battleground.

King sent several messages to Confederate headquarters complaining that there were no Southern troops left on the border to protect his family, his home, or his property. The answer was simple. There were not enough men available to help those living on the sparsely settled border. Col. Rip Ford had been ordered to move his line of defense north and east to counter a threat of invasion from New Orleans. General Bee was left with a handful of men at Fort Brown.

It was up to the big ranchers — and King had by far the largest holdings — to raise their own armies. For two years, that's just what they did. Most of the army spoke only Spanish. Between skirmishes they handled a lasso and a branding iron.

The ranchers of southern Texas prayed the war clouds would turn to storm clouds. During 1863–64, the prairies were seared by months of drought. The reservoirs, which had been so carefully dammed for emergency water supply, now dried to cracked mud. The road across the prairie was a ribbon of dust, but the cotton trains pulled by twenty-mule teams kept coming. A battle was being planned to stop them.

On November 1, 1864, word arrived that twenty-six transport ships were anchored at the mouth of the Rio Grande. Confederate General Bee at Fort Brown kept his men on twenty-four-hour alert. Every citizen of Brownsville who could get out of town did so. Henrietta's father sent his wife and two youngest children to Kentucky with friends. He was in poor health himself and feared he would slow down their travel. Instead, he and his two eldest sons rode to the Santa Gertrudis where he hoped his prayers and his rifle would help.

Only the stormy weather of November kept the troops at sea long enough for most Confederates to escape. Actually, fewer men had landed than had at first been reported, but General Bee did not wait to survey the situation. When he heard that the first of the Yankee soldiers were ashore, he decided to give up Fort Brown without a fight. He dumped the siege guns into the river and burned piles of cotton and supplies to keep them from enemy hands. Fierce winds spread the flames, and much of the town was destroyed. What remained after the fires died down, looters stole.

Six days later, the Northern army brought law and order — but only for those who were ready to surrender. The Yankee commander, General Dana, set about closing all supply routes.

"I will kill, burn, and destroy all that cannot be taken and secured," he said.

Captain King prepared to stand guard over his family. It had been two years since little Alice was born. Henrietta was now expecting their fifth child.

It was well known to the Northern officers that 124 miles away at the Santa Gertrudis ranch there was a key station on the Confederate cotton route "operated by a notorious rebel agent." Spies were sent out and returned with the message that the ranch was unprotected. It was true. Most of the ranch hands had been sent toward Corpus Christi hoping to cut off the Yankees there.

But there were spies working on both sides. Three days before Christmas, a rider raced to the Santa Gertrudis to warn King. "Captain, tonight a troop of Yankees are coming to arrest you. You must escape while there's still time."

Henrietta heard the warning. "You have to go, Captain."

"I can't. I won't leave you behind."

"Surely the Union army will not put children and a pregnant mother behind bars. When they find you are gone, they will leave us alone."

"I wish I could believe that, Etta. We must find a safer place for all of us to hide."

"You know we cannot keep up with you. In less than two months our child will be born. Where would we be safer than in the security of our own home? We have food and shelter here."

King spent a sleepless night trying to decide what was to be done. His own fate was doubtlessly either death or imprisonment for the duration of the war. In either case, he would not be able to protect his family any longer.

Henrietta was right. A carriage or wagon carrying them all would easily be overtaken by the Yankee army. Their attempted escape might so enrage the commanding officers that punishment for all of them would be severe.

It was with a heavy heart that he summoned Francisco Alvarado, the man who had built the first rough shacks at the cow camp a decade before.

"Francisco, I am depending on you. Go stay at my house and guard my family. I have to go now. I don't know when I will be able to return, but I will keep in touch."

The captain hugged each of his children and shook hands with his father-in-law. "I leave them in your care, Reverend."

"In the Lord's care," Hiram Chamberlain corrected.

At last he took Henrietta in his arms and held her close for a very long time. "Etta, Etta, take care. Be careful. I love you." His voice broke. He could not say any more.

"My prayers will be for you," she said.

She saved her tears for the moment he was out the door and was mounted on his horse. Then she broke down in sobs. For an hour she closed herself off from the rest of them. She felt so very much alone and frightened, but she knew she must not show it. There was too much to do to waste time like this. Food and water must be stored in the main house in case of siege. Siege? How did she ever think they could withstand an army with an elderly gentleman, one brave ranch hand, and a house full of children as their only defense?

There was little sleep that night. All of them crowded into one room. She placed a cot for Francisco Alvarado in the hall in front of their open bedroom door.

In the gray light of morning they heard horses pounding in the courtyard. There were yells and then an explosion as a bullet splintered the heavy wooden front door.

"Everybody down on the floor," she commanded. Then she skirted the far wall and peered out the window. Troops had surrounded the house. One man had a torch. There was only one thing to do. She prepared to go outside and meet them.

But in her place Alvarado rushed to the door and shouted, "Don't fire on this house. There is a family here."

He had no chance to say more. A bullet hit him squarely in the chest, and he crumpled to the floor. Henrietta fell to her knees beside him. A Union officer stepped across the threshold, his gun drawn.

"You've killed him. You've killed him!" she screamed.

"Your husband, Madam?" He looked down at the brown face of the Mexican who had been guarding the family. "Where is your husband, Madam?"

"Many miles from here." A child was crying. "Get out," she ordered.

"I am the head of the household now." The Reverend Chamberlain stepped forward. "You can see there is nothing and no one here you want."

"You are our prisoner. Step outside."

"I am sixty-seven years old and a minister of the gospel. I am no use to you. At least let me stay with my daughter, who you can see is soon to deliver a child."

The officer hesitated. "Then you will stay to give King the message that if one bale of cotton is carried away or burned in that warehouse of his, I will hold him responsible with his life and the lives of his family."

The officer turned and left, but he did nothing to keep his troops under control. They broke down the front door and rode their horses into the house. Mirrors, windows, and china were smashed. Clothing was snatched from trunks. There was little they left behind.

Henrietta sat in her bedroom rocking little Alice in

35

her arms, talking quietly to the others to help calm their nerves as well as her own. Hiram Chamberlain was on his knees beside her. They all prayed.

He rose and looked outside. The raiders had rounded up every mule and horse in the corral. "We should have left before they came."

"It would have been worse," said Henrietta calmly. "They might have burned everything. We are alive, and they can never destroy the land. When the Rebels hear what they have done, they will come to help."

Word did reach a small company of Confederate soldiers and loyal Mexican *vaqueros*. They changed their course and headed for the ranch. Again there was commotion in the courtyard as the Yankee soldiers regrouped, this time with the order to retreat. It was Christmas Eve.

There was little sleep for Henrietta. She must plan what was best for the family. She wished with all her heart the captain were at her side to help with the decision, but she must not try to contact him. Even though the troops had left the ranch, they might easily have left spies behind to report on her actions. No, she must guard his safety with silence. If the Union forces were so brutal in their destruction of personal property, what would they do if they ever captured the captain?

What of the children? Would the troops return? Soon she would not be able to travel herself. They must leave the ranch now. She looked around her. Broken china was scattered on the floor. The draperies had been slashed by a saber. The droppings from a horse stained the floor.

She hurried to the kitchen building separated from the house by a breezeway. She was surprised to see some slabs of bacon and butchered beef were still hanging in the pantry. The troops must have been in a great hurry. Without waking any of the others, she hauled bags of flour and fruit, whatever produce was on hand, to the courtyard.

She returned to the room where the family slept. She

lit one candle and started to pile clothing into an open trunk. Nettie was the only one to stir. When she opened her eyes to speak, Henrietta put her finger to her own lips and whispered. "Let the others sleep. We'll leave when it is light."

"I'll help," said Nettie.

The two of them packed what they could find, picking up a little rag doll that was meant for baby Alice's Christmas present. There would be no celebrating this year.

8

Henrietta was heavy and awkward. Every jolt along the hoof-pounded road caused her to suck in her breath and pray that the child within her would stay protected in her womb until they were safe, far from the enemy.

But where would they be safe? There were no stationary battle lines. Raiding parties on both sides dashed across the land at will, surprising each other at the few water holes that guaranteed their survival. Had the captain reached the border? She refused to think of the alternative.

Little Alice stirred in her sleep, cried out, then burrowed deeper in the quilt on the floor of the coach. Henrietta looked around her. All the children were sleeping, exhausted from the hours of tense suspense. Even her father's head was nodding as he held his grandson.

Four outriders, loyal *Kiñenos* mounted on the fastest horses they had been able to round up on the range, flanked the lumbering coach. The driver and his relief man were heavily armed, shotguns and revolvers loaded. But six against how many?

Henrietta had chosen to head north away from the border where Union forces might be expecting them. She had friends in the little town of San Patricio across the Nueces River, whom she hoped would take them in. It would be an act to test the loyalty of even the closest friend, to feed so many extra mouths and to harbor the family of one of the most wanted men in Texas. King had almost singlehandedly kept the Confederate army along the border supplied with food, mounts, and ammunition. Without the captain's help and organization, the Rebels might have given up their cause in this part of the country long ago.

Henrietta had not misjudged her friends. All four of the children were put under the care of Dorcas Delano, a white-haired, ample-bosomed grandmother of thirteen, who seemed to have a magic way of curing problems with laughter. She was employed by the Henderson family, who in the past had often bought prime breeding stock from the King ranch.

Henrietta was bundled off to bed for a much needed rest. The last person she remembered seeing before closing her eyes was her father on his knees with his head bowed in prayer. They were safe now, at least for a while. Henrietta let herself slip into a deep sleep.

On February 22, 1864, Henrietta gave birth to a healthy baby boy. Searching for a name for the infant, she chose one familiar to all as a leader, brave and dedicated to the cause she shared. The child was named Robert E. Lee King.

As soon as she was able to travel, she sought a place where her husband might be able to reach her, maybe even to join her. The city of San Antonio was well guarded by Confederate troops. Again she boarded the coach with her father and five children. She had no money, but a name that was trusted and known throughout the South.

They moved into a small rented house and waited.

39

Messages were finally received that the captain was safe — at least as safe as one could be in the midst of war.

The hard-riding, tough group of commandos he was with was known as Richardson's Company of Black Hatted Rebels. The entire fighting force was made up of loyal *Kiñenos* commanded by his own ranch foreman, Captain James Richardson. King served as a private at his own request.

The next year he spent most of the time in a saddle, joining forays against the Union army and, even more importantly, riding protective patrols at the front of long columns of wagons loaded ten feet high with bales of cotton. Instead of heading directly south to Brownsville and across the Rio Grande to Matamoros and market, the wagons were forced to detour west and then south.

All King and Kenedy steamships had been sold to Mexicans to keep them out of the hands of the Union army. In fact, everything that could be converted into cash in this southern tip of Texas ended up across the Rio Grande.

When the formal end of war came on May 24, 1865, the Yankees were surprised and angry. When accounts were settled across the treaty table, there were no spoils of war to be taken. Southern Texas fared much better than the rest of the Confederacy during Reconstruction. Yet, there was still a grave fear both Henrietta and the captain shared: that the ranch itself would be confiscated. Officially, all property now belonged to the U.S. government.

Richard King wrote to U.S. Gen. Giles Smith, who commanded the Brownsville territory, asking for presidential pardon and the return of the ranch property. His letter was ignored for several weeks. No one was available to take over the ranch. The innovations already developed in cattle breeding and ranch management required someone with experience. Only planning on a tremendous scale, with capital to weather the bad years, made these experiments possible, experiments that were changing the future of the Southwest.

Finally, with the intervention of Rip Ford, who had been appointed commissioner of parole (even though he had fought on the side of the South), a clear title to all the King property was finally delivered.

King at once went to San Antonio with a carriage loaded with gifts for the family. There was a toy for every child, even baby Lee, who immediately became the center of attention. For Henrietta he had somehow managed to purchase a beautiful pair of diamond earrings.

She looked at the sparkling gems nestled in their velvet jewel box. She hesitated. "It would be vain of me to display such indulgence."

"Dear Etta, for once think of yourself. Promise me you'll wear them."

Henrietta looked up into the eyes of her husband. She felt his tenderness and love, and her own love flowed back. It seemed so important for him to hear that promise. He had been gone so long. Her heart had ached; now it was full. She slipped the dainty jewels out of the box and put them on her ears. They embraced. No words were needed to bring them together.

Henrietta kept the promise to wear the earrings always, but in her own way she preserved her wish for the unpretentious. She had a jeweler cover the stones with dark enamel. Only her family knew she wore a modest fortune in perfectly cut flawless diamonds.

9

Henrietta's hope that family life could now settle into a normal pattern was not to be. She found herself as frequently without a husband by her side as during the war. There was much to be done to reorganize the ranch and freight business.

Richard King first set about buying back the river freighters he and Kenedy had owned before the outbreak of the war. They were in poor condition, but with a minimum of repair, they were put into service immediately. There was no competition, and although commerce on the border was not up to normal, profits were easy to come by.

War had brought a scarcity of beef to the densely populated states of the North and Middle West. The same war had brought an almost incredible increase of untended cattle onto the prairies of Texas. Herds drifted across unfenced plains at will. Cowboys had been riding the range rounding up the enemy, not cattle, and natural breeding had doubled the sizes of the herds. Now all that was needed was the manpower to drive them to market.

A five-dollar steer on the range was worth twenty dollars in Kansas City. The peak of the cattle boom spread out over the next thirty years.

Thousands, not hundreds, of steers were rounded up and marked with the Running W brand to be driven north to the rail sidings. The trail bosses, called "Kansas men," were the most important people on the ranch, and they were paid well. Each trip north took two months or more. The cattle were driven slowly so as not to wear them thin before market. To keep the broad highways of grass open, King bought up more and more land so that he controlled miles of right of way. But it was always his hope that rail lines could be laid right up to the border of his range.

King rarely took part in the entire drive, but he was on hand for every roundup and he supervised cattle selection. Bulls were slaughtered for hide and tallow. The best bulls were kept for breeding.

More than branding was needed to keep King's cattle separated from the others. He started an extensive program of fencing his range. The first corrals were built of roughly chopped mesquite laced with wet rawhide which dried to steel strength. About 300 miles of this fencing was laid out. In the next century, some 800 miles of net wiring was strung along the boundaries. Barbed wire was rarely used on the King ranch because of possible injury to the animals.

Henrietta continued to share responsibilities at the Santa Gertrudis. When imported Shorthorns were bought to stock the Encino section, she was at her husband's side inspecting with interest the smaller, chunkier dark-red animals.

"They seem to be easier to handle," she observed.

"Until you put two of them together," King chuckled.

The biggest problem they had was cattle rustlers. Being so close to the border and without the manpower to ride patrol on all fences, herds of a thousand or more could be stampeded across the Rio Grande into Mexico.

43

There was no way to reclaim the property. Some of the ranchers south of the border openly bragged, "Those *gringos* are raising good cows for me."

The army could not help. Therefore, King armed the *Kiñenos* and spread his men over a thin line from one horizon to the other. These were Mexican-Americans asked to fight their Mexican neighbors, but loyalty was never a problem.

The captain never carried a revolver, but he was rarely seen on the range without a shotgun filled with buckshot. The cannon was still mounted on adjustable blocks in front of the headquarters house, but it was there for effect more than for use.

Holdups were anticipated, particularly at the end of a trail drive when cash was transferred to the owner, frequently in the form of gold bullion. Often a heavily guarded wagon would be sent ahead. Only Henrietta knew of the cleverly concealed strongbox beneath the false set of floor boards in the family carriage.

The answer to robbery was speed. The captain rode the fastest horses in the corral, each bred for racing. Relays were posted along his route. More than once he outran bandits while carrying a fortune in cash. Not that he couldn't trust others to handle deliveries and arrange contracts, but danger brought excitement to his life. The war years had marked him. There was to be no settling back in a rocking chair.

Henrietta's father died in his sleep the year after the war ended. Her stepmother returned to her home in the East, but her three sons, Henrietta's half brothers, stayed on at the ranch. The house had been renovated and enlarged. Henrietta was surrounded by family, but when the captain was away, the house seemed empty — no matter how many sat down to the family table.

When the captain did return from a trip, it was always with presents for "my pets." Henrietta tried to forbid indulgence. She failed. No matter how hard she tried to avoid flamboyance, the captain thwarted her.

Henrietta decided to leave the children behind one time and accompany her husband on a business trip to New Orleans. The King name had spread beyond the state of Texas. This was made clear when the owner of the hotel greeted them as royalty, with the entire staff lined in military precision at the front desk. The captain decided that his immediate want was food. Giving orders that their luggage be taken to their suite, he led Henrietta directly into the dining room. Waiters snapped to attention.

A seven-course meal, complete with the finest steak available, was ordered. When the captain noticed that Henrietta was having trouble cutting her meat, his temper flared.

He shoved back his chair and bowed formally to his wife. "Stay right here, Etta. I'll be back in a moment."

Henrietta recognized by the stamp of his boots that something was about to happen, but she was afraid that by leaving she would arouse more attention.

When King returned she was relieved to notice that his anger seemed to have disappeared, that he even smiled and started to discuss a proposed continuation of their trip to Kentucky. However, a short time later, Henrietta noticed a commotion at the door of the dining room. Waiters were arguing with waiters.

King rose from his chair, reached across the table to grasp the far corners of the tablecloth, which he gathered up, plates and all, and deposited on the floor with a mighty crash. The waiters at the doorway pushed forward, trays in hand, and set an entirely new seven-course dinner on the empty table.

King had left the hotel, gone across the street to another restaurant, and had ordered the dinner to be served to him at the hotel.

While he chuckled in satisfaction, Henrietta burned

with humiliation. The captain had forgotten the high spirit of the young girl he had first seen aboard the *Whiteville*. She rose, marched out of the room, had her luggage removed to the sidewalk, and hired transportation to take her to the train station. The captain was left to enjoy his dinner alone.

10

Henrietta encouraged travel as part of her family's education. In 1867, she visited Virginia. Henrietta proudly took their three-year-old son Robert E. Lee King to see his namesake. The general was delighted to meet the little boy and complimented him on the fine suit he was wearing. "Only trouble is I don't care much for the color."

Henrietta suddenly realized she had dressed him in blue, the color of the Union army uniform, not the gray of the Confederates.

Again the general showed much interest in the ranching business. He was surprised at the detailed accounts Henrietta was able to give on the size of the herds recently sent to market and the purchase of a hundred Kentucky Durhams to upgrade a select herd of range cows.

In 1870, when Nettie King was fifteen, she was enrolled in a Presbyterian girls' school in Henderson, Kentucky. Ella and Alice were sent to Mrs. Cuthbert's Seminary in St. Louis, which was more easily accessible to transportation from Texas. Henrietta enjoyed visiting them. The captain was usually too busy for any extended traveling, but he urged her "to take off when the spirit moves you."

This was one luxury she allowed herself. The spirit moved her quite often. She would have the carriage packed up and order the driver to take her to the nearest rail line.

She enjoyed traveling. Although many strangers tried to arrange an introduction, knowing she was the wife of one of the country's wealthiest men, she preferred to keep to herself and enjoy the scenery without conversation.

She had never been one to depend on others, except for the captain. When he was away she was lonely. Now that the children were almost grown, there was a feeling of not being needed. One of those empty days in late fall she was sitting in the parlor, a book of unread poetry open in her lap.

Suddenly, the captain burst into the house, just as suddenly bringing life and energy to her quiet world.

"Etta, what am I going to do when I'm not fit to look over this spread? Dick wants to grow crops, not livestock. Lee loves the ranch but wants to invest our profits in Eastern industry. No one has the same vision for the future of this land as you and I, Etta."

She nodded. She had long shared his concern for the future of the ranch, but she tried to put his mind at ease. "There's plenty of time to put things in order."

"No, darn it Etta, there isn't."

He paced the floor and pulled on his long black beard, which had grown to touch the second button of his shirt. He was wearing his usual dark broadcloth coat and wrinkled pants. It was well known that when the captain appeared with one pant leg in and one pant leg out of his boot tops that the barometer was falling, a storm was brewing. Henrietta wanted to calm that storm, but she had to know what had triggered his mood.

"Where were you this morning?"

"I just rode in from the west pasture by the Ball ranch. The grass is thin. Any fool should have known better than to keep a young herd on those rations."

"Let me get my bonnet. I'll ride out with you in the buckboard."

"It's hellish hot out there, Etta."

"I don't mind. I want to see for myself what the drought has done."

He grinned. "Not many a partner would be so willing."

He reached down to fix his pant leg. The storm was over.

As the years piled on the captain's shoulders, his health failed. He suffered from gnawing pains in his stomach. Food was no pleasure any more, but he forced it upon himself to keep up his strength. He had no intention of giving up the ranch management, not until he had picked his successor and trained him firsthand. His sons were not ready.

Never once did he give a second thought to how his wife might carry on without him. Surely the ranch would legally become hers, but this was not the generation to give management to one wearing skirts.

He met the man who was eventually to shoulder these responsibilities in a law court.

Richard King and Mifflin Kenedy had brought joint action to end the nuisance of trespass along a certain road which passed through both their properties. The lawyer opposing them was a newcomer to Corpus Christi, trying his first case in Nueces County. His name was Robert Justus Kleberg. Much to everyone's surprise, King and Kenedy were beaten due to the skillful handling of the case by Kleberg.

That evening, the young lawyer went to bed early but was wakened from sleep by a loud knocking at his door. When he answered the summons, there stood Captain Richard King. Kleberg, uncomfortably self-conscious in his night shirt, stammered a welcome and ushered his unexpected visitor into his rented parlor.

King wasted no words. "I'm looking for a good lawyer. How would a retainer of five thousand a year suit you?"

It took a moment before Kleberg understood what had been said. Five thousand was considerably more than he could expect to earn his first year practicing in a border cow town, so why was he hesitating?

With a grin he put out his hand to shake King's. "Accepted. When would you expect me to start, sir?"

"Right now. My team is outside, and if you can find your pants, I aim to leave now. We can talk business on the drive out."

It took a lot of miles for King to outline some of the work he planned on turning over to the young lawyer. He explained he was still anxious to add to his land holdings, but he had no intention of turning over hard cash until titles were cleared. During the earlier Mexican War and even since the War Between the States, some tracts had been abandoned. Wills had to be checked and relatives tracked down in different parts of the country to find the rightful owners before offers to purchase could be drawn up.

"I've found a good lawyer is as valuable as a branding iron in putting my stamp on what I own. I just want you to tell me when I can move my fences."

It was dawn before King pulled leather to stop the team in front of the two-story ranch house. He went in and wakened his daughter Alice. "I've brought a visitor and we need some coffee."

She didn't ask why the kitchen help had not been summoned. Her father often impulsively called on her. When she returned with the coffee and a plate of sugar cookies, the stranger was introduced. They were both to remember that meeting, although brief. Alice was nineteen, Kleberg twenty-seven.

Business talk went on for another hour before Kleberg was shown to a bedroom. With only a bare outline of the work ahead of him, he figured he would be busy for the next six months. King would be getting a bargain for his $5,000.

Kleberg immediately became involved in the ranch business, but it was the "paperwork kind," as King put it. Only the captain and the range bosses knew what prime beef cattle and horse flesh were roaming the prairie of the Santa Gertrudis. Most of the young lawyer's time was spent sorting over records in the county courthouse.

11

Alice's two older sisters were married, first Nettie to Major Atwood in St. Louis. The newspaper reported that "the hotel parlor was transformed into a regular garden of flowers . . . The presents were the handsomest ever given to a St. Louis bride." Several large cases filled with solid silver valued at over $10,000 were part of the bride's trousseau.

Three years later, in 1881, Ella King was married to Louis Welton, a merchant in St. Louis. This time Henrietta had her wish that the wedding be held in their home on the Santa Gertrudis. It was a simpler ceremony, although the house overflowed with guests.

When the couple left on their honeymoon, the quiet closed in very suddenly. The boys were away at school. Only Alice was left to share the house so far away from town.

One of the Northern newspapers, again reporting on the fabulous King family, noted that visitors arriving from Corpus Christi entered the ranch gates a good ten miles before arriving at the headquarters house. The ice man from Brownsville (yes, the captain had imported ice-making machinery to preserve his groceries) had at least thirty miles of driving across ranch land before he reached the back door. It was a country of itself, almost as isolated as if castle walls and moat surrounded it.

No wonder Henrietta frequently made the trip to the city to visit her daughters. As grandchildren began arriving, there were added reasons.

The captain was not able to get away as often, but in one of his letters he made his feelings clear. "See that none of Papa's pets wants for anything that money will buy." In another letter his words were, "Life is short and why be so mean as not enjoy ourselves now?"

His own wish for improved health could not be bought. He was almost in constant pain, but he continued to keep informed on all ranch activities. His *vaqueros* watched for the familiar figure, the bearded sunburned face under the dusty black hat, the boss riding the spring seat of a light, slat-bottomed buckboard, a Winchester rifle and a bottle of Red Eye whiskey at his side.

What he saw didn't cheer him. A long drought had withered the plains. "Where I have grass, I have no water. And where I have water, I have no grass. Cattle won't wander far from water, so we have lush pasture they won't touch. I'm in a hell of a fix," he wrote nineteen-year-old Lee, his youngest son and the one on whom he hung his highest hopes.

Young Lee loved the land. Now if he could just be taught the business of turning it into a profit. "Land's no good unless you do something with it," King had said many times.

Lee was in St. Louis enrolled in a business college. King was never one to value schooling over "range learning," but he admitted college was doing Lee no harm. "It takes a heap of figuring to keep accounts straight and know when to buy and sell." But King was impatient for him to return to the ranch for his real education.

"It will take a lifetime of learning to keep things

going at the present rate of growth. No time to reinvest in some strange business far from home." That was what Lee had been suggesting.

King felt that Lee would have to take charge soon. He was ready to hand over the reins, but during the latter part of February, a telegram came from St. Louis. It was sent by a doctor stating that Lee was gravely ill.

"Can't be," said King. Without waiting for further word, Henrietta, Alice, and the captain rushed to Lee's side. The day after their arrival on March 1, 1883, Lee died of pneumonia.

It was a stunning blow to both parents. Each handled it differently. Henrietta tried hard to reconcile the loss by a faith in her church. It was no use. She had been strong during the months she had carried him in her body. She had bravely given birth to him attended only by strangers, not even knowing whether her husband were alive or dead. Now she wept and stayed away from the ranch, the ranch that Lee had so loved. Henrietta dreaded facing memories.

The captain returned to his land broken-hearted. He tried to ease the pain with work. Alice and Richard, Jr., were with him. A month after the funeral, he made a decision to sell the ranch.

Almost immediately, offers were received. A British syndicate was formed with the power to purchase all stock and land. Before a final settlement was made, the captain sent a wire to Henrietta.

Her answer was clear. "We have lost a son, but we mustn't lose our land. Remember what General Lee told us, 'Buy land. Never sell.' I will return."

That was the last time there was talk of breaking up the ranch. As if to brighten the picture of the future, the rains came. The range turned green, and the number of beef was higher than ever. Henrietta sat next to the captain on the driver's seat of the wagon as they rode the fence lines.

That summer, young Richard was engaged to be married to Miss Pearl Ashbrook. As a wedding gift, they received a deed to "40,000 good and well-watered acres," and while away on their honeymoon, the foundations of an elegant home were laid to add to the gift.

Young Richard was not as spoiled as facts would hint. Henrietta, more than the captain, had seen to that. Dick had ideas of his own, though, about how he would convert the pastures to farm land. Cotton and oranges were to be the cash crops. The captain did not approve of the change. In earlier years, when he was in robust health, there would have been a rip-roaring fight over the plans to set plow to land, but he had no energy for fighting. There were no sons to take over the complex management of the Santa Gertrudis. He turned to the young lawyer Kleberg to handle the marketing contracts and to keep track of the monumental bookkeeping tasks of the ranch.

The captain was tired now. Henrietta could tell by the slump of his shoulders, the pain in his eyes. She urged him to leave the ranch for a few weeks to see another doctor, a specialist in San Antonio. He agreed only after arrangements were made to take care of business while he was in town. He was to meet with other cattlemen in the area to discuss the selective breeding program he had started with the Durham bulls. Those meetings never took place.

When the Kings arrived at the Menger Hotel in San Antonio, Doctor Herff was there to greet them. The diagnosis was not good. King was suffering from cancer of the stomach in its terminal stage. The doctor advised him that drinking was radically shortening the time of life left to him.

He made no promises until Henrietta spoke quietly, "I need you a while longer, Captain."

King jerked himself up and out of bed. "Give me my pants and boots. I aim to last that while longer."

From that day on he abstained from drinking, but little time was left. On April 14, 1885, he died. He was sixty-two years old. Henrietta was left a widow at fifty-three.

12

Outwardly, Henrietta had seemed to live in her husband's shadow, but those closest to her knew that was not the case. She had strong convictions of her own. Her judgment had helped make most of the family's decisions and many of those involving ranch business.

The captain's will bequeathed everything to her "to be by her used and disposed of precisely the same as I might do were I living."

There were to be three executors of the estate: Henrietta King; Mifflin Kenedy, their old friend and former partner; and a Corpus Christi banker, Perry Doddridge. Shortly after the will was read, Kenedy and Doddridge decided to decline the job as executors "thinking the interest of said estate to be best subserved thereby."

Henrietta was in charge. Robert Kleberg and the ranch foreman who had been herd boss for many years helped set the official appraisal of the estate. In round figures, Henrietta found she was left half a million acres of land and half a million dollars of debts.

At the time of the captain's death, the cattle boom of

the early 1880s had collapsed, leaving the prices of live-stock and land depressed. Robert Kleberg, fresh from a law office with little knowledge of the animals on the range, found himself with horrendous problems. Henrietta in her quiet way was the key person who kept the whole enterprise going until the lawyer could be trained as rancher.

The captain had planned well. Each section of land had its own overseer. The crew handling the breeding of horses and mules was separate from the cattlemen. There were also large numbers of sheep and hogs on the ranch, but each boss had his own job and specialty.

Henrietta sat at the big desk in the office going over ledgers. During that first year of depression, very few cattle were sent to market. They were left to breed on the range. There was always a demand from other ranchers for prime breeding stock from the Santa Gertrudis. This was what kept the ranch financially solvent. Cash was used to buy more land when the prices were low.

Robert Kleberg learned in a hurry. For four years, he had been a part of the King family. Since the first morning he had arrived at the ranch, his friendship with Alice had grown and matured into a deep love and respect that would last a lifetime. Their courtship had been interrupted many times with business crises and then, of course, the captain's death.

Finally, on June 17, 1886, they were married. It was a quiet celebration, made quieter since the passing of the larger-than-life founder of the ranch.

Alice, the most devoted of the King children, insisted that her mother not be left alone for the summer. Henrietta was invited to join them on their honeymoon trip north. She accepted.

When they returned to the ranch, the three of them set about organizing the work ahead. Alice was given the domestic responsibilities of the house and overseeing the feeding of the ranch crews. Henrietta, with the steady and increasing help of her son-in-law, set about clearing the debt and expanding the ranch. She continued the captain's practice of moving the fence lines past the horizon.

James Doughty, an old Texas stockman, took Kleberg on as an anxious pupil. Ramon Alvarado and "Jap" Clark were the two expert horse bosses. They brought Kleberg up-to-date on what bloodlines the King ranch was trying to develop. There were others, too, who had spent their lives on the ranch and had sons and daughters to perpetuate the loyalty they felt for "La Madama" and, in turn, the new boss man.

When Kleberg first arrived at the ranch, he spoke no Spanish. Now he set about learning the language and gaining the respect of the Mexicans. The old captain had been called with a kind of tongue-in-cheek affection "El Cojo." Their new patron became "El Abogado," the lawyer.

One of the first jobs was to clear out the big headquarters breeding pastures. The cattle were largely unworked, unbranded, and as wild as any on the range. The pasture was choked with thorny brush which was removed. Then, wire fencing was strung to make the enclosures smaller. Each corral had its water hole, and only a regulated number of animals were assigned each section.

Henrietta sat in on most weekly conferences held at the headquarters office or on the front porch when the weather wasn't too dry and blistering hot — a fact of life during most of the summer months.

"Water is what we need. We've come up with nothing but salt water wells on the Norias section," Kleberg complained. "The United States Department of Agriculture is experimenting with some rain-making equipment, but there's no guarantee it will work."

"I think we should try it anyway," said Henrietta.

The rain-making effort consisted of a discharge of explosives into the sky. It made a spectacular noise, but no rain fell on the Santa Gertrudis.

"I think if we could go deeper with the wells we could find fresh water," Henrietta suggested.

"It'll cost money to bring in heavier equipment, and there's no guarantee it'll work," Kleberg argued, but they both agreed that something drastic had to be done immediately. Cattle were dying by the hundreds, and the *Kiñenos* were sent out with skinning knives to salvage the hides.

A heavy drilling rig was hauled in from Kansas and set up in the southernmost pasture. Every day, Henrietta and her son-in-law drove out to visit the rigs. Instructions were given "to keep right on boring until your drill comes out on the other side of the earth, unless of course you find water sooner."

On June 6, 1899, a clear column of pure artesian drinking water poured out on the ground at the rate of seventy-five gallons a minute. The result was of immense importance to the future operation of the ranch — and to the entire state.

Cattle would roam only a limited distance from a water hole. In between, the grass was left untouched. Henrietta's foremen estimated only about a twentieth of the land on the ranch had been used by the herds. She remembered the captain's words, "Land isn't worth anything unless you do something with it."

So the well-drilling crews were kept busy bringing in other wells.

Transportation of cattle was the next problem tackled by the new management. The cattle drives were over. The range was now crisscrossed with fencing even the King money could not clear. A railroad was the only answer, a line laid right up to the pastures. Robert Kleberg was dispatched to find interested investors. While he was away, Henrietta was the one sitting behind the big desk in the office, unless she was out in the pastures. She didn't ride out as she had before with the captain, but she spent much of her time on a buckboard wagon, covering miles between the various separate parts of her property.

Yes when she was satisfied everything was under

control, she would travel north to the cities where she had close friends and family. Here she was equally at home in the regal surroundings her wealth could well afford. Even though she never showed off her riches, Henrietta in no way could be described as a typical pioneer homesteader of the Old West, not any more.

She had lived through the excitement and danger of Civil War, range war, and border war, but her toughness was within. The old captain had fit the picture of a rough character with a habit of command. He had often said to her, "I have to make them think I'm a man eater. If I don't they'll kill me, or steal me clean." Times had changed.

Henrietta was strong but gentle. She brought the polish of poetry reading and music to her parlor, which was visited by many of the country's most noted people. She had become a *grande dame* of note far beyond the pastures of Texas, whether she liked it or not.

Not long before Robert and Alice Kleberg were married, the big frame house was enlarged for the third time. A second-story, ten-bedroom addition to the back of the house was built, and the lattice-railed outside galleries were extended along the entire lengths of both floors. Henrietta's favorite chair was placed by the front door. She was always dressed in black. The only jewelry she wore were her black enameled diamond earrings and a broach engraved with the captain's likeness.

More trees were planted for shade. The old cannon was still parked by the carriage driveway, now paved with crushed white shells.

Guests were invited to the house, both to conduct business and for purely social pleasures, although the party atmosphere was apt to be somber. No hard liquor was allowed on the premises, and ladies were to appear for meals in "freshly changed dresses." A British noblewoman visiting the ranch once appeared at mealtime in a riding outfit. Henrietta promptly asked her to change.

Three signal bells were sounded before every meal.

The first was a notice to "clean up." At the second bell, guests assembled in the parlor, and at the third ringing, Henrietta would lead the procession out of the main house to the dining building.

Henrietta always presided at the head of the table, her son-in-law at the opposite end. Alice, seated close to her mother, helped fill the role of hostess by always knowing the names of guests and directing the conversation toward their interests, if Henrietta had not had time to be briefed in advance. After supper there were often songs at the piano in the music room. Card playing was not allowed.

A year after Alice and Robert were married, their first child, a son, was born. During the next ten years, four more children — three girls and another boy — were added to the list of Henrietta's grandchildren.

Alice chose to spend the last month of each of her pregnancies in Corpus Christi, where she was attended by Dr. Arthur Spohn, the family's doctor. He was more than a physician to them, being considered one of the family. He had well earned their trust and affection.

In April of 1888 he had saved the life of Willie Chamberlain, Henrietta's half brother. Willie was bitten by a rabid coyote at the ranch. Dr. Spohn rushed with his patient on the fastest ship across the Atlantic to France in time to have the great Louis Pasteur administer his newly discovered vaccine. Willie Chamberlain was one of the first patients to be given the treatment. Henrietta would always be grateful to the Texas doctor. In later years, she gave a large sum of money for a hospital dedicated in his name.

These were some of the happiest years of Henrietta's life. She enjoyed watching the grandchildren grow up on the same land and in the same house as her own family. From their earliest infancy, the Kleberg children took an active part in ranch life. The girls, as well as their brothers, were at home on horses, sometimes accompanying their father hunting deer, turkey, or quail on the ranch's great pastures. Henrietta's only sorrow was that the captain had not lived to see another generation enjoy the life he had so abundantly provided.

When the children were of school age, one by one they moved into the family mansion that had been built in Corpus Christi. They stayed only for weekly classes and returned to the ranch every Saturday.

Henrietta spent much of her time there, too, in comfortable elegance, but she disappointed many of the town's matrons by not entering into the social whirl of entertaining. Her hospitality was reserved for close friends and family, yet she delighted in keeping abreast of all the town news. One morning she was particularly aggravated when Alice gave her a detailed account of what had been happening. She made no complaint, but the next morning at breakfast Alice asked the cook, Anita, to bring her the newspaper. Anita looked nervously at Mrs. King, then the floor.

"I send for one," she answered.

"That won't be necessary," Henrietta replied. She then faced Alice. "I'm sitting on it. This morning *I'll* read the news first and report it to *you* later."

In spite of a few tales of Henrietta's eccentricities, there seems to have been little friction or argument over her demands. Alice perhaps had to have the soul of a saint to permit her mother to make so many family decisions, but in reality family conferences were where most of the decisions were made. There was love and respect between mother and daughter, who in reality were so very different.

Obviously, a woman of Henrietta's age living in her generation could not have handled the business of so gigantic an empire without tremendous help, but legally the property and all livestock on it belonged to her and without her encouragement to step ahead in bold agricultural experiments, these innovations would not have taken place.

Her cattle were the first to be dipped to cut down

Texas fever transmitted by ticks. Her pastures were the first to be reseeded with new kinds of grass. Prickly pear cactus was processed for food after burning the thorny outer skin. A system of irrigation and water storage units were developed when drought frequently cut back the grass.

The most important part of the ranch work involved scientific experiments in selective breeding. The Santa Gertrudis raised more horses for the United States cavalry and more mules for Southern farmers than any other ranch in the country. Its cattle production dwarfed all others. And it was Henrietta more than any other member of the family who insisted on adding to the already enormous sprawl of land within her own boundaries.

A map of the entire southern tip of Texas was hung on the wall at headquarters. The checkerboard pattern of land acquired covered most of five counties. Henrietta now owned slightly more than a million acres of land. The question was how to put it to the best use.

_13_

By the turn of the century, telephone and electric wires had been strung many miles across the prairie to ranch headquarters. Hot and cold running water was now tapped into the new bathrooms. A gasoline-powered car was parked in the carriage barn.

How to improve rail transportation was still the major problem. Robert Kleberg had not been able to interest any of the big railroads to invest in a spur line. The ranch's closest shipping station by rail was the little town of Alice, named by Henrietta for her daughter. But there were no rail lines south of Corpus Christi. The formerly important border town of Brownsville, where Henrietta had first met the captain on the banks of the Rio Grande, had now sunk into sleepy isolation. If they couldn't get anyone else to build the railroad, the answer was to do it themselves.

With Henrietta's blessing and with much of her capital, a corporation was set up for the purpose of constructing, maintaining, and operating a rail line south across the Nueces River, 160 miles to Brownsville.

Foreseeing a great boom in land values and trade, they planned for the future. A town site was selected, which would border the rail line at a convenient distance of three miles from ranch headquarters. Henrietta was involved with every bit of the planning. The town was appropriately named Kingsville.

The railroad was financed by capital in the form of land bonuses to the builders. Henrietta's original donation was one-half interest in more than 75,000 acres, in addition to the right of way across her property.

The construction work was completed within a year. The first excursion train northward from Brownsville made its run July 4, 1904. Flags waved, cannons boomed. A brass band played.

Henrietta rode over in her carriage to the new town site of Kingsville to wait for the train, the first ever to move over the prairie that had been her home for almost half a century.

When the train came into sight she was as excited as any of the shouting, clapping children of her family. She stood by smiling. "Thank goodness it is here."

In respect of Mrs. King's wishes, the train did not run on Sundays. The first complimentary pass was issued to Mrs. H. M. C. King. Scheduled time for the passenger run of 158.06 miles from Brownsville to Corpus Christi was nine hours. Stagecoach service took forty hours.

Henrietta's grandchildren were also issued passes. On Friday afternoons, the general manager of the line would order a caboose hooked to an engine, and when school let out the Kleberg kids had their own train waiting for them to take them to the ranch for the weekend. They raced for the privilege of climbing up the ladder for the choice high seat with the cupola window. Their horses would be waiting for them at the station to take them the last three miles to the big house. Sometimes Henrietta would drive over in a carriage to meet them.

She liked to watch the smoking, chugging engine clatter over the tracks.

Surveyors were busy in Kingsville. Eight hundred and fifty-three acres were divided into 226 city blocks. Fifty dollars was the price of an ordinary lot. Choice corner locations went for five hundred. Farm lots were also put up for sale, but Robert Kleberg was determined to control sales and discourage speculators.

Every deed contained a clause strictly forbidding the sale of liquor. This was probably the only Western town without one saloon. Families came to stay. One year after the first lot was sold, the town built on a cow pasture had a population of nearly a thousand.

The Kingsville Publishing Company, owned by Henrietta, published a weekly paper. The Kingsville Ice and Milling Company, owned by Henrietta, brought an ice factory to town, and the Kingsville Power Company, built mostly with Henrietta's funds, brought electricity to town. She was also the sole owner of the Gulf Coast Cotton Gin Company as well as Kingsville Cotton Oil Mill Company. She made wise choices in selecting people to work for her, and every division of her business enterprises made money.

She was also gracious with gifts. Property was first given for a Presbyterian church, and Mrs. King's lumberyard provided the materials for construction of a handsome building. She gave property as well to the Baptists, Methodists, Episcopalians, and Catholics. She also donated the land and all the funds — about $75,000 — for a twenty-two-room brick schoolhouse.

Although other settlements sprang up along the rail line, the carrying of freight in the form of livestock, not passengers, was its reason for being. Near the home of Caesar Kleberg, a cousin of Robert, the ranch built the largest set of shipping pens in the world. Finally, the captain's dream had come true. Now it was a lot easier to get steers to market than on the hoof across dry and dusty trails that the early Kansas man had blazed.

He would also have been proud of the cattle being shipped from these pens. By 1915, Kleberg had established the largest purebred Shorthorn and Hereford herds in the United States. Since 1886, he had matched the ranch's original Longhorn cattle with these two British breeds. While he watched them make a better quality beef, he also watched them sicken and die in the heat of Texas summers. Either they had to return to the scrawny but healthy kind of cattle the captain had first started with or find another breed to stock the prairie.

A drastic decision was made: a few Brahman cattle from India were introduced into the herd of Shorthorns. These huge animals were often vicious and hard to handle. They also lacked the quality of fine beef, yet they were used to the climate. Their loose, ugly hides enabled them to stand great heat, and they seemed to have a strong immunity against disease and could fend for themselves on scarce pasteurs.

The following spring a few crossbreeds were born. One promising bull calf was kept for further breeding. Henrietta asked to be driven to the pasture to look at the new animal. "I've seen drastic changes in the land, but I never expected you could alter the conformation of an animal so. It doesn't seem exactly right that this wasn't the plan of God almighty."

"And who's to say it wasn't, Grandma?" answered Dick Kleberg, who had become his father's right-hand helper.

She nodded. "You're right."

What Henrietta had seen was the first of an entirely new breed of cattle, which was officially recognized as Santa Gertrudis. The Klebergs had gone one step further than the captain. They had proved themselves to be breeders, not mere multipliers of cattle. They tailored cattle to their own requirements, not as trained geneticists, but as practical ranchers. The young lawyer, who had been put in charge of a puzzling enterprise, had done much to carry on what the captain had started in 1853.

14

As the years passed, Henrietta's health suffered but not her spirit. She walked with a cane now. People could tell by the rate of its tapping just what her mood was for the day, just as the captain's trouser leg out of his boot had forecast the barometer in earlier days.

The big house was always full of family and friends and sometimes strangers to her, but her hospitality was always generous. Another change to the ranch house had added a third floor with dormers to the front section. It was indeed an imposing house set in the middle of a stark landscape.

But on January 4, 1912, Henrietta, now nearly eighty years old, saw this home, which represented so much of her life, burn to the ground.

The house had been full the day before. A group of visitors from the East had been hunting on the ranch. They had left for the train at Kingsville early in the evening. Only guests Mr. and Mrs. Jeff Miller remained with the Kleberg family and Mrs. King.

Dick Kleberg's bulldog wakened the two sons sleeping on the first floor. About the same time, the Millers on the second floor discovered smoke and flames. Without waiting to dress, they dashed outside along the porch gallery to the front of the house to arouse the rest of the family. Flames had already destroyed the rear stairway. The Millers were forced to climb down the outside porch to escape. Mrs. Miller fell and broke two ribs.

In the meantime, Henrietta had dressed herself and had the presence of mind to throw a few valuables in a satchel and pack her "medicine bag," as she called it. The front stairs were still in tact. She made her way outside calmly while the others rushed about accomplishing little. She counted the faces around her. "Where's little Alice?" she demanded.

Little Alice, who was now eighteen, had slept through all the commotion. It was her brother Al who ran back into the house to save her.

Robert Kleberg returned to the smoky office and vault in the southwest corner of the house. He bundled up some of the records and cash before having to retreat.

Two of the ranch hands tried to move the grand piano outside, but Henrietta stopped them. "Leave it. Let nobody get hurt. We can build a new home. We can't replace a life."

Alice, now entirely awake, ran to the kitchen building and rang the farm bell. Every hand around headquarters came running, but the flames had already burst through the roof. The fire was visible for miles across the prairie. As the crowd backed away from the blistering heat, someone suggested to Henrietta that she go rest in the commissary.

Years later her grandson, Al Kleberg, recalled the moment. "I can see her now, all dressed in black with a little black bag in her hand. She turned and threw a kiss at the burning house."

Within a few weeks, a one-story structure was hastily erected as temporary housing until a new home could be built. Henrietta could have remained in Corpus

Christi, but she returned to the little house that must have reminded her of the honeymoon cottage without a pantry.

Henrietta left the planning of the new mansion to her son-in-law, but not before giving him this advice: "Build a house that anybody can walk in in boots."

Only mighty fancy boots would have felt at home in the lavish mansion constructed on the same rise of land by the Santa Gertrudis River. Built of hollow tile and stuccoed concrete, it was a massive fireproof fortress. The design was part Mexican, Moorish, and California Mission.

The main house had twenty-five rooms, each with its own fireplace, and wide cool verandas. A grand living room displayed murals of the Alamo and scenes of the livestock and wildlife of the ranch. The dining hall could accommodate fifty guests. The floors were made of mesquite boards cut on the ranch, polished and pegged with ebony. Tower windows were fitted with Tiffany-designed stained glass.

It was elegant but severe. There was no trace of the graceful, relaxed comfort which the old house had enjoyed. Yet every modern convenience was included. A ten-car garage was added to the carriage house, and a new dairy barn was built.

15

Across the Atlantic, World War I had started, but there was real fighting much closer at hand. The troops of Pancho Villa, Emiliano Zapata, and Alvaro Obregon were engaged in a duel for power in Mexico. They were financing their battles by systematically raiding the ranches north of the Rio Grande of supplies and cash. More than a dozen people were killed on the King ranch alone.

On March 9, 1916, a telephone call came from Kingsville warning the Klebergs that a band of raiders was on their way to the big house. Immediately, a defense was organized. High-powered rifles, ammunition, and field glasses were gathered and carried to the roof. A search light was hastily rigged atop the tower.

Trustworthy *Kiñenos* were issued guns, and the battle lines were drawn. Henrietta insisted on being taken on a personal tour of the defenses. When she saw that all possible precautions were being taken for their defense, she expressed satisfaction. "Everything seems to be in order. I'm going to bed."

In the middle of the night, a raiding party started for the King ranch, but when they saw the private army waiting for them, they wheeled their horses around without a shot. It was a happier ending than the morning Henrietta had to face the Yankee raiding party.

During World War I, the management of the ranch was turned over to twenty-one-year-old Robert Kleberg, Jr. His father's health was impaired with palsy, and his older brother had almost died of a ruptured appendix. Bob already had plenty of first-hand training and had just graduated from the School of Agriculture at the University of Wisconsin.

With Henrietta's blessing, he took complete charge of the properties. Bob wanted immediately to return to his grandfather's idea of land use. His bias for the branding iron and prejudice against the plow was argued forcibly with his father. The senior Robert was in favor of selling more tracts of land along the railway right of way to farmers.

"Biggest fool thing you could do," said Bob. "Land's too sandy, water too scarce."

Henrietta listened. It sounded like words from the captain. She had actively given up making decisions about the ranch several years ago, but still her word, her approval, was sought. With all her years, she had by far the most intimate and longstanding knowledge of the land. She stood behind her grandson now. No more farm land was sold.

It was time, she knew, to draw up her will. The Santa Gertrudis headquarters, including 30,439.23 acres and the great house, were turned over to her daughter Alice. But instead of depleting her land holdings, she continued to add to the ranch.

The very next year she took title to 21,122 acres surrounding a large salt lake. It furnished the much needed salt for her cattle. She also purchased a large section of dry pasture, known as sand country, but oil had been discovered nearby and there was a chance — yes, a good chance — that exploratory wells would bring in their own production.

In appreciation for the many years of service Robert Kleberg had given to the ranch, she deeded to him an interest in any future petroleum developments. It proved a rich gift to Robert and Alice Kleberg's children.

Henrietta survived all of her grown children except Alice. In April 1918, a message brought the news of Nettie's death. Four years's later, the captain's namesake, Dick, died of a stroke.

At age ninety-two, Henrietta King's memories of Texas were a complete history of the state. She had lived to see her home in the wild, outlaw country gentled with luxurious comforts. Yet the pastures stretching past the horizon had not changed, and the herds enclosed in the miles of fencing still required the same attention during roundups and brandings as they had when they roamed wild across the range. Much had changed. Much had stayed the same.

Her death came calmly in her sleep on March 31, 1925. The word was spread by newspapers all over the world. She had become a symbol as a lone survivor from a lost chapter of history.

Friends and family gathered to pay tribute. All the *Kiñenos* came, some riding horses two days and a night over ranch property to arrive in time for the funeral.

The procession from the great house to the cemetery in Kingsville, named Chamberlain Park in honor of Henrietta's father, was more than a mile long.

An honor guard of the ranch's cowboys, nearly 200 of them, wearing their range clothes and riding quarterhorses branded with the familiar Running W mark, flanked the hearse.

When the casket was lowered into the earth, each of the riders came forward single file to canter once around the open grave, their hats down at their side as a salute to Henrietta King.

Among the lavish flower wreaths was a simple Running W woven of wildflowers. Henrietta would have been pleased.

GLOSSARY

apprenticed — worked under a master craftsman to learn a trade

barometer — an instrument to measure atmospheric pressure; in this case, an indicator of change

brine solution — a heavy salt solution used for pickling and preserving foods

bullion — raw gold or silver before being made into coins

chaparral — a thicket of shrubs and thorny bushes

coquettes — girls or women who flirt to get the attention of men

cosmopolitan — having broad and worldwide interests; not limited to local habits and customs

croup — a sickness which causes coughing and difficulty in breathing

cupola window — a dome-shaped window

dormers — windows set upright on a sloping roof

eccentricities — a person's odd or unusual habits

flamboyance — a showy, extravagant manner

fore — toward the front

geneticists — those who study traits and characteristics passed on from parent to child

grande dame — an older woman of great dignity

mooring line — a line that holds a ship to the shore

mull — a thin, soft material

palmetto — thick area of palm-leaved plants

saber — a heavy sword used by cavalry soldiers

scuppers — the openings on a ship's side which allow water to run off the deck

sorrel — a light brown color

spoils of war — goods or territory taken by force in war

spur line — short, connecting line for a railroad

straits — narrow waterways which connect larger bodies of
     water
tallow — solid fat taken from the natural fat of cattle
trousseau — a bride's outfit or collection of clothing and
     materials
vaquero — a Southwestern cowboy, usually of Mexican origin
transients — people who drift from one place to another